How to Analyze People

Art of Deception, Hypnosis, Mind Control
and Subliminal Persuasion

Abraham Travis

Table of Contents

Introduction

W e have seen that the ability to persuade is one of the most crucial ingredients in our dealings with people if we want to influence others and do not want to be relegated to camp follower's role for the rest of our lives.

The greater we can persuade others, the better we will be in whatever field we are pursuing, be it social, business, or recreational. At first glance, some of the tactics we have looked at may seem manipulative, but we soon see that persuasive people are sensitive to others' needs and feelings when examined in greater depth.

And to remain in roles where they continue to have the most significant influence, they need to generate high levels of loyalty and respect. Doing this requires sensitivity, integrity, and excellent communication skills.

It is not sufficient to simply persuade people to follow you once or twice. To gain influence, we need to establish ourselves as persuasive on an ongoing basis. This requires trust, credibility, and a high degree of empathy for the needs of others.

We have seen the result of fear generated persuasive techniques used by dictators and despots the world over. In the long term, these tactics always crumble and leave behind deep bitterness and hate.

Chapter 1:

How can you persuade or influence someone else way of thinking?

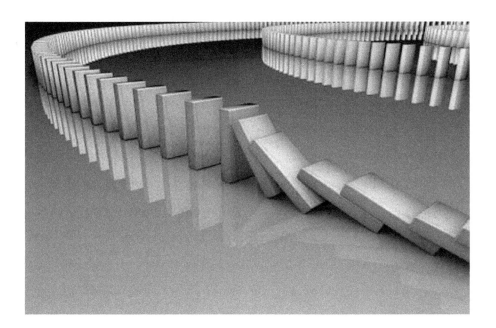

Persuading People

P ersuading people is the last part of the three-step process to successfully manipulate anyone. Persuading is what you want to use after you have planted the seeds of manipulation. Manipulation is where you offer the solution, and persuasion is where you get to tip them over the scale so that they say yes. Manipulation is the part that mostly relies on verbal techniques, whereas persuasion is a series of verbal and physical techniques that you use to really get the person on your side and agreeing with you.

Overcome Their Trust Issues

People are always going to have trust issues. One of the best ways to persuade someone is to learn how you can overcome someone's trust issues so that they trust you. While this can sometimes take weeks or even years for some people, master manipulators are great at earning trust in a matter of seconds. It works through being charismatic, staying confident, and holding authority in your conversation. When you are able to lead the conversation, be friendly and open to the person you are talking to, and really get them to warm up to you, it becomes a lot easier for you to persuade them to work in your favor. This is the very first part of persuasion that you should practice every single time, no matter what drives them, what the solution is, or what you want to gain from the experience.

Know Your Product (Or Purpose)

When you are trying to manipulate people, you are going to have to overcome objections. They are going to ask questions, have concerns, and want to make sure that you aren't just trying to pull their leg. Even if you are, it is important that it doesn't look like you are. Having a clear understanding of your product or your purpose is a great way to ensure that you can provide answers and explanations for any objections in a moment, without missing a beat. When you have to stop and think about why someone should agree with you, you ultimately give them several moments to think about why they should not agree with you. The faster you answer with your reasoning, the more likely they are going to agree with you. This shows that you are educated, you have a purpose, and you know everything that is needed to about either the product or the purpose behind what you are asking for.

Here is an example of a conversation where you overcome objection by knowing your purpose thoroughly. Imagine you are trying to get someone to cover your shift because you don't feel like showing up for work that day. If you simply say you don't feel like showing up, they are not likely to cover your shift. However, if you have a really good reason as to why you can't show up, they are more likely to make it work out. Here is an example of the conversation:

You: "Hey Peter, can you cover my shift today please?"

Peter: "I don't know, I'm busy today, though."

You: "But my car broke down and I don't have a way to work."

Peter: "Can't you take a bus?"

You: "One doesn't run past my house, and I don't have money for a taxi. I really need my shift covered though so that our boss doesn't get angry with me, I had to miss a shift last week too for my doctor's appointment."

Peter: "That sucks. I don't know, though."

You: "Please, it is only a 9-12 shift so you won't be there long. Catherine is already doing most of the work, so all you will have to do is show up for the three hours and get paid."

Peter: "I guess so."

You: "It's basically like getting paid to sit there, and I know you were asking the boss for extra shifts last week. Can you take it?"

Peter: "Okay, fine."

Here, you collected evidence and provided reason as to why Peter needed to cover your shift. You didn't only appeal to your need, but you also appealed to his need. Ultimately, you want to make your offer sound like they need it more than you need them to take it. When you can make it sound like it is good for them, the person you are persuading is far more likely to agree.

Stay Calm and Confident

In addition to being able to appeal to someone's need to trust you and to being charismatic and authoritative in a conversation, you also need to know how you can stay calm and confident. There are going to be many times where you feel nervous, or like you want to break your character and express emotions other than calmness and confidence. If you do, however, you are not going to be able to persuade people. Instead, you need to emanate calmness and confidence the entire time.

When people are starting to object to what you are asking, remain calm and confident. Assert why they are in need and stay positive in your position. Do not start getting desperate or pushing for them to agree with you or side with you. Instead, continue to be calm and confident as you swiftly work through the different stages of manipulation. At some point, you will earn their trust and they will come along with you. If you break character, however, they may begin to see through your actions and realize that you are only trying to manipulate them and that you aren't actually paying attention to their concerns or needs.

This is the same during informative parts of the conversation as well. When they are asking questions, give the answers with clarity and confidence. Be extremely assertive as to why they need what you are offering, and never waiver. When they ask about a certain feature, explain what that feature does with complete confidence, even if you aren't completely sure that you understand it yourself. The more you can remain confident, the easier it is for you to keep people confident in you and what you are talking about. Then, they will be more likely to agree with you and take what you are offering.

Manipulate Your Body Language

As you know, body language is massive. Most of us can read it on a basic level as a basic survival skill. However, many don't realize that they are reading it. Furthermore, some will realize they are reading your body language and they may also be well-versed in what different signals mean. For both reasons, you need to manipulate your body language to comply with what you are trying to accomplish. For example, if you are trying to sell something and you want to be seen as confident, you cannot be expressing body language that shows that you are nervous. This will lead people to wonder what you are trying to hide and will cause them to not be trustworthy in you or your offer. Alternatively, if you are feeling desperate for their compliance and you show this through your body language, they are going to see your desperation and believe that you are not genuinely trying to help them, but rather that you are desperate to help yourself.

When you are working to manipulate people, always use confident body language. The only time there would be an objection to this rule is if you are playing the victim. Then, you need to use body language that looks as though you are feeling attacked or otherwise pressured by the person you are trying to manipulate. In general, however, you want to stand with a tall posture, with broad shoulders, and with your head parallel to the floor. Do not turn your nose up at people, and do not look up at them by turning your head downward, either. Instead, look at them straight on, smile, and practice so that you can respond without skipping a beat.

Techniques for Persuasion

Learning about the traps of persuasion will give you new awareness for when they appear in sales messaging you read. The greatest advantage? Your cash stays in your pocket. It literally pays for you to understand exactly how sales representatives and marketers offer you items that you don't really require. The following are some persuasive techniques that work on a subconscious level.

Outlining Impacts Thought

Let's say you're thirsty, and someone hands you a glass of water not-quite full. "The glass is half full." An optimist would "outline" the reality of your glass of water in that way. Outlining is used as an approach to modify how we classify, connect, and attach meaning to every aspect of our lives.

The headline "FBI Operators Surround Cult Leader's Compound" creates a mental picture strikingly different from another version of the headline for the same story: "FBI Specialists Raid Small Christian Gathering of Women and Children." Both headlines may convey what happened, however, the selected words affect the readers' mental and emotional responses, and therefore direct the impact the target events have on the article's readers.

Outlining is employed by apt government representatives. For example, representatives on both sides of the abortion debate refer to their positions as "pro-choice" or "pro-life." This is intentional, as "pro" has a more positive association to build arguments on. Outlining an event, product, or service this way unobtrusively utilizes emotional words strategically to persuade individuals to see or accept your perspective.

Creating a convincing message is as easy as selecting words that summon strategic pictures in the minds of your audience. Indeed, even with neutral words surrounding it, a solitary stimulating word can be powerful.

Reflecting as Persuasive Strategy

Reflecting, often called "the chameleon effect," is the act of replicating the movements and nonverbal communication of the individual you want to persuade. By mirroring the actions of the individual listening, you create an appearance of empathy.

Hand and arm motions, inclining forward or reclining away, or different head and shoulder movements are types of nonverbal communication you can reflect. We, as a whole, do this without much thought, and now that you're becoming aware of that, you'll notice not only yourself but others doing it, as well.

It is important to be graceful, thoughtful about it and allow just a couple seconds to pass between their movements and you reflecting them.

Highlight Scarcity of a Product or Service

The concept of scarcity is often employed by marketers to make products, services, or associated events and deals appear to be all the more engaging on the grounds that there will be restricted accessibility. The belief is that there is a huge amount of interest for it if availability is scarce. For example, an ad for a new product might say: Get one now! They're selling out quickly!

Again, it literally pays to know that this is a persuasion strategy that you will see everywhere. Consider this concept the next time you settle on your buying choice. This principle triggers a feeling of urgency in most individuals, so it is best used when applied in your marketing and sales copy.

Timing Can Bolster Your Good Fortune

Individuals will be more pleasant and accommodating when they're mentally exhausted. Before you approach somebody for something they may not otherwise participate in, consider holding back until they've recently accomplished something mentally challenging. Consider making your offer toward the end of the workday, for example, when you can get a colleague or collaborator on the way out of the office. Whatever you may ask, a reasonable reaction could be, "I'll deal with it tomorrow."

Enhance Compliance to Acquire a Needed Result

To avoid cognitive dissonance, we all try to be true to how we've acted in the past. A reliable technique businesspeople use is to shake your hand as they are consulting with you. We have been taught that a handshake equals a "sealed deal," and by doing this before the arrangement is really sealed, the businessperson has taken a step to persuade you into believing the deal is already done.

One approach to employing this yourself is influencing individuals to act before their minds are made up. Let's say that you are roaming downtown with a companion, and you decide you want to go see a movie at the local theater; yet, your companion is undecided. Compliance can come into play if you begin strolling toward the theater while they are still thinking about it. Your companion will probably consent to go once they realize you are strolling in the theater's direction.

Attempt Fluid Discourse

In the natural flow of our speech, interjections and reluctant expressions act as fillers when we need a moment to think or select the "right" word, for example, "um" or "I mean," and obviously the newly pervasive "like." These fillers have the unintended impact of making us appear to be unsure and doubtful and, in this way, less convincing. When you're certain about your message, others will be more effectively persuaded.

If you have trouble finding the right words at the right time, practice some free-flow association every day in front of the mirror for 60 seconds. You can add it to your morning ritual, or you can do it while having a shower, like I usually do. Basically, your goal in these 60 seconds is to jump from one topic to another very quickly, by associating words; do your best to avoid "um," "like," or other fillers.

Example: The water on my back right now is so hot, it reminds me of the hot weather in California. I love Cali; I like the food there. Mexican food is so spicy and hot, like Mexican women. I remember Marcella, that one Mexican girl I met last time I was there; she was probably the only blonde girl from Mexico. She was blonde like a Swedish model. I've never been to Sweden, but I've heard it's cold out there...

And so on, until you get to 60 seconds without pauses or interjections. Once you reach that point after some practice, you can aim for 120 seconds. Once you've done that, the next step is to practice this game with other people. You don't need to go on for a full two minutes straight, but while you're talking to someone, you can go on a tangent for 20 seconds and practice the free-flow association skill. You'll practice and improve tremendously, while they'll be wondering "This guy is interesting. I really want to know what he's going to say next..."

Chapter 2:

Difference between Influence and

Persuasion

Influence

While mind control can help in some situations, having natural influence can be better in many instances. Influence is much more subtle and often non-verbal.

Heck, just by having influence, you'll be grouped in with other players in the big leagues. After all, influence is not just an advantage; it's a necessity for most leaders and persuaders. The charisma, charm, and expertise displayed through influence are associated with top tier qualities. But how do you achieve it?

Methods of Influencing Individuals

There are more methods of influencing another human being than one might be aware of. One proven method is that of mirroring or copying the behavior of another person. This takes the form of a type of body language in reverse. Instead of using your body to convey a message, you use their body language and play it back to them. By using the same motions, head positions and similar facial expressions, it has been proven that you can create a more harmonious relationship with another person. Obviously, this makes that person more vulnerable to you being able to influence her, and this may be advantageous if you need to persuade that person to take a particular course of action. The problem with mirroring, as it is referred to, is that if the other person detects you are doing it then it has the opposite effect to that which was intended, and you can lose influence altogether. If you feel this is a tactic that may be useful to you, and I don't want to persuade you here, then you must be at your most discreet. The perception that they are being copied will lead people to conclude that you are mocking them.

Another method that uses a somewhat similar strategy is that of social proof. In other words, if everyone else is doing something then you should too. The fashion industry has traded on this since it began. It is not for no reason that we find that fashion follows trends from year to year. Few people like, or can tolerate, being the odd one out. If straight hair and tight jeans are in this year, then nearly everyone will be wearing their hair straight with tight jeans. Of course, all you need to do to really reiterate your marketing position is get a well-known celebrity to wear tight jeans and straighten their hair, and you are away. This phobia of breaking the chain of peer acceptance is very powerful. That is why many advertisements use expressions like "nine out of ten customers found that such and such a product worked wonders for their health". Immediately they have established that this is the thing that most people are doing and the fear of being seen as out of place will kick in automatically. Creating a crowd mentality of one kind or another is an almost guaranteed method of persuading people in a particular direction. It is a method that has been used by politicians, dictators, and religious promulgators, almost since those professions came into existence. Once you grasp how this very basic human characteristic works and how widespread it is, then you are able to capitalize on it. If you wish to persuade a child to do something, then, first of all, you should convince that child that all his friends are doing the same thing. This simple technique relates to the workplace as much as it does to the playground.

Probably some of the most adept people at persuasion are politicians, and they love to use this strategy to persuade others. Unfortunately, they are weak when it comes to recognizing when this method is being used against them, and that is why you will so often see politicians changing their point of view if they feel that there is a majority going the other way. We need to be aware of this and make sure that our own paths are not influenced by group pressure. As stated earlier in this book our integrity is an important factor in maintaining influence, and this may evaporate if we are perceived to sway too much in the direction of the crowd.

Influencing others is also a matter of being able to pick out other key influencers in a group and harness their power. If you are working with a group of people, it's a waste of time to try persuading one of the less influential members of something if they are only going to be swayed by someone else, coming along with a contrary line of thought. Instead, you need to focus your efforts on the most influential people in the knowledge that if you can win them over to your idea, then the battle is half won.

Now when it comes to influencing people, most of us tend to make the same mistakes. We underestimate ourselves and don't work towards it.

As we've just mentioned, you can cosmetically seem influential by placing your qualifications in your office for everyone to see, but cosmetic influence can only get you so far. In high stake, public situations, influence comes from your network. Who you know and how well?

That's why you'll see everyone from politicians to CEOs name dropping people they know in obvious or subtle fashions. If you have correspondence with someone such as Bill Gates, as someone who works in the software or tech industry, your credibility and influence have double the effect. This is often overlooked or considered as a secondary, automatic response to gaining influence. However, if you use your intent to gain this type of influence early, you'll establish yourself as an experienced persuader early on.

That said, it's not every day Bill Gates, or other such high-ranking individuals are available to connect with. Or are they? One of the best-kept secrets by expert persuaders is their ability to connect with others.

Their networking tactics are often not talked about since that's how they derive a large chunk of their influence. That said, their tactic is very simple and doable. *You simply ask.*

In the age of social media, most influencers are looking to connect and build their networks. They're just waiting for brave, worthy persuaders to contact them.

For them, your connection is a valuable way to get their word out there and reinforce themselves as authority figures in their respective fields. For you, it's your ticket to getting one of the easiest credibility boosts.

It may not seem easy or natural the first few times you connect, but you'll soon see how easy it is to connect with influencers around the globe. Just start with a hello and a free valuable offer and take things from there.

There are a few things you should keep in mind, however. Some *dos* and *don'ts* when it come to influencing people. After all, if your employees, friends or loved ones notice how you're trying to control them in any fashion, it might prove to be troublesome, *at best*.

<u>The secrets to influencing people the right way:</u>

Ask for influence

No one is going to hand you influence on a silver platter, or any platter for that matter. You need to proactively achieve it. Networking is the most beneficial skill you can pick up. It not only gains you influence but helps give you access to expert, established persuaders and learn from them. If you're too scared to ask for influence, no one will consider you worthy enough to possess it.

Don't say no

No is a negative word in most situations, particularly when it comes to persuading people. While most of us can recognize opportunities and say yes to those, most don't realize how they might be saying no to someone else. Through our negativity, we can be answering for the person. So, as you've learned in this book, keep your message positive and always lean towards *yes*.

Don't influence strangers

Influencing partly works because of a connection between two or more people. Others need to trust your words and empathize with you in order to get influenced by you. That's why you see a lot of big religious evangelicals and motivational speakers form a connection with their audience before diving into their teachings. The first step should always involve friendship and a genuine one at that. As said, you're not trying to manipulate people, so don't give anyone the impression that you're trying to use them.

Listen to what others have to say

As we've discussed previously, listening to others is a definite way of connecting with them. If you're not paying attention, it's unlikely you'll leave a good impression on anyone, especially when you're dealing with the big dogs. To show you're listening, ask related questions and stay involved in the conversation.

Don't talk about yourself

This is one of the biggest mistakes rising persuaders make. Making a conversation or situation about yourself isn't in line with persuasion, but borders on manipulation. Not to mention, it becomes a major turn off. Only talk about yourself as much as the other person directs.

Once you start applying these simple tricks, you'll notice a dramatic change in how people, big or small, treat you. Blending different types of influences according to your strengths is how you make yourself a credible persuader.

Simple Advice for Dealing with Other People

It is good to avoid arguments. This is the way to obtain the most from it.

Make others aspire for a nobler, higher motives.

Begin in a friendly manner and act in a friendly way.

Show respect for the other person and other person's opinions. Never judge or condemn them.

In case that you are wrong, admit is simply, quickly and emphatically.

Let the other person do the talking. Be a good listener.

Let the other person think that it is she or he who have brought forth a new idea.

Try to be empathetic. Put yourself in the perspective of another person.

Sympathize with the other person's thoughts, feelings, and desires.

Be charming in presenting your ideas.

Be challenging.

Persuasion

When you hear about the word persuasion, there are probably a lot of different things that end up coming to mind. Some people will think about some of the advertising messages that they see all over the place each day, the ones that are trying to get the audience to purchase a product that is for sale. Others may think about politics and how a politician who is running for office will try to use persuasion to get you to vote for them rather than the other person. Persuasion could be the car salesman who wants you to go for the newer model, the friend who wants you to go see a specific movie, and so much more.

Finding a good definition for persuasion can be a little bit difficult because there are just so many different types of persuasion out there. Persuasion is something that we see on a daily basis, but it is a really powerful force in our daily life, and it can have some major influences on society as a whole. Whether we are talking about advertising, news, mass media, legal decisions, or even politics, we are talking about things that will use the power of persuasion to get the viewer or the other person to hopefully do what the messenger wants.

With so much persuasion found in the world around us, it is common for us to think that we should be immune to the powers of it. Sure, there are hundreds of advertisements around us each day, and we do not go out and purchase every product that is being shown to us, but this doesn't mean that we are never persuaded to do things in our lives.

Sometimes it is easy to avoid the power of persuasion. If the message is something against our beliefs or if we do not want the product at all, and sometimes even when the sales pitch is too pushy, we can see right through the persuasion, and we will avoid doing what the other person wants us to do. This is easy to do when the signs of persuasion are very noticeable and out there.

But what happens when the signs of persuasion are harder to see and recognize? Are we really able to recognize all forms of persuasion and how are we going to respond to some of the persuasion techniques that seem to sneak up on us? The way that we are going to respond to some of the methods of persuasion will vary based on a variety of factors that are going on in our lives, who is delivering the message, and so much more.

Any time that we think about persuasion, it is likely that the negative examples are the ones that are going to show up first in our minds. However, there are quite a few times when persuasion can be a positive force. Our parents convincing us to go to college, going and hanging out with some friends at a new place to eat, and even public service announcements that ask people to recycle can all be examples of persuasion that is used in a positive manner.

So, now that we know a few of the examples of persuasion, it is time to learn a bit more about what persuasion is really all about. Basically, persuasion is just a process in which the communicator is going to try to convince others to change their behaviors or attitudes regarding an issue through a message. This message is sent out through free choice, so the viewer can pick how they want to respond to the message (they are not being forced to respond in any particular way to the message), but the message is often geared towards convincing the viewer that it is best to act in a certain way.

There are some key elements that are present in the art of persuasion. Some of these key elements include:

When it comes to persuasion, we are going to use symbols such as sounds, images, and words to get the message across.

To be considered persuasion, the message needs to be a deliberate attempt to influence others.

Self-persuasion is the key to all of this. No one is going to be coerced into behaving in a certain way, and they do have the right to choose. For example, when you are watching an advertisement online, you are not forced to go down to the store and purchase that item for sale. You can make a choice about whether you would like to purchase that item or not.

There are a lot of different ways that you can transmit a persuasive message. You can do it nonverbally and verbally through the radio, internet, and television and it is also possible to do this through face to face communication with others.

Chapter 3:

When is Persuasion considered a form of bad manipulation?

D ark psychology is a construct of human consciousness, and the study of the psychological nature of people to prey on others are driven by their psychopathic, psychopathological, or deviant criminal tendencies, without any particular purpose.

Dark psychology is based on instinctual and biology drives. All people have the potential to take up dark psychology to victimize their fellow humans or other creatures, but the majority chooses to restrain or redirect this urge. However, a few decide to act on these evil impulses.

Dark psychology is a psychology facet created to try to understand the thoughts, perceptions, and feelings that go through the minds of those who succumb to their dark impulses and take on predatory behavior. Dark psychology first assumes that there are some 99.99 percent rational, purposeful, and goal-oriented reasons behind this behavior. The rest, only 0.01 percent, is thought to be just brutal victimization of other people without any purposive intent or any other reasonably defined dogmas based on science or religion.

One fact the dark psychology ideology stresses are that in every human mind is a region that enables the individuals to commit atrocious acts without any single driving reason, in what is called the dark singularity theory. The theory posits that all people have a reservoir of malevolent intent towards other people ranging from having fleeted minimally obtrusive thoughts to a pure psychopathic deviant behavior that lacks any rationality. The range of malicious intent covers simple ideas to incredibly psychopathic behavior. The range is called the dark continuum.

As such, dark psychology is the condition and the study of all that makes us who we are in regard to the dark side. You will find it across people of all nations, all cultures, all backgrounds, all religions, and all ages. From the moment a person is born, he or she will possess a dark side that some have termed as pathological, criminal, evil, or deviant. This dark side is the reason some people will commit heinous acts not driven by the need for money, power, retribution, sex, or any other known purpose. They will gladly injure or violate others for no reason at all. Sadly, every human being has this wicked tendency inside.

The part of the universal human psyche that allows for and impels predatory behavior is also addressed in dark psychology. It addresses the fact that these behavioral tendencies lack predictability, lack rational motivation, and lack obvious rational motivation. In doing this, dark psychology assumes that this universal human condition is an extension of the evolution process. You see, since we evolved from animals, and based on animal instincts and predatory tendencies, our behavior should be based on three primary instincts: aggression, sex, and a survival need. These three instincts seek to ensure procreation, survival, and protection of territories.

If you have watched a nature documentary and seen a lion chase down and tear apart an antelope, you cringe and feel sad for the antelope, but the reality is that the brutality fits the lion's evolutionary need to self-preserve by getting food. Although the lion will have submitted to its psychopathic tendency by choosing the weakest, the youngest or the females of the group, the reason for doing this will be to increase its chances of survival by reducing its probability of suffering injury or death.

Natural selection, evolution, and animal instincts seem to dissolve when you consider the case of humans. We are the only species on the planet that preys on others of its kind without any good reason, driven by inexplicable motivations. We do it for other reasons besides food, survival, procreation, and territory. There is, therefore, something dark about the human psyche that causes predatory behavior. The unknown thing is anti-evolutionary, and all people on the face of the earth, all who have existed before, those alive now and those who will come, will have this dark side.

Unfortunately, the dark side of the human being is unpredictable. Humanity is unpredictable because it is the person that will act on these dangerous impulses, and on the length of time, an individual will go having entirely negated his or her sense of mercy. This is the reason why some people perpetrate heinous acts like rape, torture, and murder, and you would be surprised to learn that there is no apparent reason behind this behavior. Vandalism of property, watching horror movies and playing violent video games also fits into this dark psychology definition, though on the milder side of the dark continuum.

Chapter 4:
Cognitive Dissonance and
Manipulative Psychological Abuse

How to Utilize Manipulation

Manipulation is a technique used by everyone at some point in life. If you think about it, you start learning to manipulate as a small child. For example, you start taking on extra chores and a week or two later, you ask for a new toy. Your parents feel compelled to give it to you since you have been helping so much. This same strategy works in adulthood too. In fact, there are numerous financial and emotional benefits that come with properly using the different manipulation techniques.

Manipulation essentially plays on people's emotions. However, to be effective, you need to be able to successfully do this and be able to read people. There are several techniques that will allow you to do both of these. Once you are good at both, you will find it much easier to get what you want every time that you need something.

Fear and Relief

This is a common manipulation technique that you have used at some point without even realizing it. This involves using another person's fears to get them to do something for you. You essentially cause some type of fear and let it build. Once the person is getting to the peak of their emotion, you relieve that fear. At this point, they are vulnerable and much more likely to do something for you.

This is a technique that is used by employers on a regular basis. They make it seem like a person might lose their job, eventually give them reassurance and then ask that employee to do something. Of course, the employee does it because they feel they have to do it to keep their job.

Reading Body Language

When you can determine a person's state of mind, it is easier to control it. Sure, you can ask them what they are thinking, but more often than not, they will not be honest. However, you cannot fake body language. If you can read body language, you will know exactly what a person is thinking.

For example, you are trying to persuade someone to give you money. Their words are saying "no," but their body language shows that you are breaking them down. As long as you can read this body language, you will know that you can push further and get the money that you need.

You want to see how they are holding their posture, if they are still or moving and where they are looking when they are talking to you. All of this tells you exactly what they are thinking despite what they are actually saying.

Guilty Approach

This is a manipulation technique that humans have been using on each other since the dawn of time. When you make a person feel guilty about something, you make them vulnerable, and vulnerable people are easier to persuade. It is best to use this technique on people you know on a personal level.

This is because you can find something that you know will induce some guilt. This technique makes it possible to slowly plant your desires. Then, when you suggest an idea, they tend to go with the flow on a subconscious level.

Use Your Looks

Humans, whether they admit it or not, tend to be shallow when it comes to looks. This is just a fact and even if you recognize this trait in yourself, you cannot help it. If you tend to be good looking by society's standards, it is much easier to persuade people to do things for you.

Play the Victim

This is another common manipulation technique that really works. When you play the victim, you essentially make people feel sorry for you. When people feel this way, it is natural human instinct for them to want to correct what they did to make you feel bad. When they are in this vulnerable state, you can essentially make them do anything. Now, this technique will not work on all people. You have to choose those that are naturally more vulnerable and less tough. The tougher people usually will not fall for the victim act, so use this technique wisely.

Prey on Their Feelings

This technique can work on all people but is easiest with those who are already emotionally vulnerable. With this technique, you essentially make people fall for you to get them to do what you need. When a person falls for someone, they are less likely to make rational decisions. Instead, they make choices on an emotional level. When someone is thinking with their emotions, they are much easier to control.

Bribery

This is one of the oldest manipulation techniques in the book because it is almost always effective. When someone feels as though they are being rewarded for helping you, they are almost always going to help.

For example, you do not feel like doing the finance report at work. Find someone who can do it, ease into the conversation and then offer them lunch if they will do the report.

Make sure that you are confident when you are asking since it is harder to say "no" to a person who is smiling and confident. Keep your tone neutral and make sure to follow through with your bribe. Once this works once, it will be much easier to persuade that person in the future without even having to bribe them.

Psychological Tactics to Influence People to Do as You Wish

You do not have to be the CEO to motivate individuals to hear you out. The mental research proposes there are a lot of approaches to inspire individuals to do what you need—without them acknowledging you've influenced them.

I've gathered together 11 science-supported systems for inspiring individuals to like you, to purchase stuff, and to give you what you're after.

Change the environment to inspire individuals to act.

"Priming" is an effective mental marvel in which one stimulus delivers an associated reaction to another stimulus, frequently unwittingly.

One example, referred to in the book *You Are Not So Smart*, found that members playing an ultimatum game selected to keep more than half of a cash prize for themselves when they were situated in a room with business-related items like a satchel, a calfskin portfolio, and a fountain pen versus when people were asked to connect items with unbiased associations, like a backpack, a pencil, and cardboard box.

Despite the fact that none of the members knew about what had happened, the business-related articles may have primed those subjects of the game to be more selfish.

This strategy could possibly work when you're dealing with somebody one on one, as opposed to meeting in a gathering room, consider assembling in a coffeehouse, so your audience is less disposed toward animosity.

Help propel somebody's objectives to motivate them to help you.

Analyst Robert Cialdini says one approach to impact individuals is to conjure the correspondence standard, invoking the concept of reciprocity. Essentially, you help somebody with something they require, so they feel obliged to furnish a proportional payback.

What's more, when gratitude has been expressed for your assisting, Cialdini exhorts saying something like, "Obviously, it's what accomplices accomplish for each other," rather than "It's no issue," so they have a feeling that they're relied upon to do likewise for you.

Copy individuals' non-verbal communication to inspire them to like you.

Whenever you're attempting to awe an enlisting administrator or to offer a protestation of your love, attempt unobtrusively mirroring the way they're sitting and talking—they'll presumably like you more.

Researchers call it the "chameleon effect": we tend to like discussion partners that copy our stances, idiosyncrasies, and outward appearances.

Talk rapidly to get a contentious rival to concur with you.

How you impart your thoughts can be as vital as the substance of your contention.

There are recommendations that when somebody can't help contradicting you, you ought to talk quicker, so they have less time to process what you're stating enough to respond.

Expectedly, when you're conveying a contention that your audience concurs with, talk more gradually, so they have an opportunity to assess the message.

Confound individuals to inspire them to agree to your demand.

The "disrupt-then-reframe" (DTR) procedure is a subtle approach to inspire individuals to participate. One review found that when experimenters visited individuals' homes offering note cards for philanthropy, DTR helped them profit when they were offering eight cards for $3; as in the DTR fashion, they told individuals it was 300 pennies for eight cards, "which is a deal."

Analysts say that DTR works because it upsets routine manners of thinking. While attempting to make sense of what number of dollars 300 pennies turns out to, individuals are occupied. Thus, they simply acknowledge the possibility that the cost is actually "a deal."

Approach individuals for favors when they're drained to inspire them to participate.

A ready personality may express some uncertainty when tasked with a demand. However, somebody who's drained or occupied will probably be less unsure and will basically acknowledge what you say as genuine.

So, if you want to request that a colleague assists with a venture that will, as far as anyone knows, just take 60 minutes, it's best to solicit toward the end of the workday.

That way, they'll be depleted from the day's assignments and won't have the mental vitality to understand that the venture will likely take up a greater amount of their time.

Show a picture of eyes to inspire individuals to carry on morally.

In one review, individuals were more compelled to tidy up after themselves in a cafeteria where they saw a picture of eyes than when they saw a picture of blossoms. The review creators say that eyes normally invoke the idea of social investigation.

Regardless of whether you're attempting to avoid littering or urge individuals to give back the books they obtain from the workplace library, it gives individuals the feeling that they're being viewed.

Utilize nouns rather than verbs to inspire individuals to change their conduct.

In one review, individuals were solicited for responses to two adaptations of a similar question: "How imperative is it for you to vote in tomorrow's decision?" and "How critical is it to you to be a voter in tomorrow's race?" Results demonstrated that members in the "voter" condition will probably cast their ballot at the polls the following day.

This is likely on the grounds that individuals are driven by the need to have a place, and utilizing a noun fortifies their way of life as an individual from a group.

Panic individuals to motivate them to give you what you require.

Collected research proposes that individuals who encounter uneasiness followed by a liberating sensation, as a rule, react emphatically to subsequent demands. For instance, individuals who heard an undetectable policeman's shriek while crossing the road were more likely to consent to take a survey than individuals who didn't hear anything.

This phenomenon is justifiable and understood in light of the fact that their subjective processing assets were preoccupied pondering the potential threat they experienced, so they had fewer assets left to consider the light demand (i.e., the survey) that was recently postured.

Focus on what your bartering associate is gaining to motivate them to take your offer.

While bartering, accentuate for your associate what they're going to gain instead of what they're losing by taking your offer. For instance, if you're attempting to sell a used automobile, you ought to state, "I'll give you my car for $1,000," rather than, "I need $1,000 for the car."

That way, your associate could understand the offer as being made from an "I'm about to cut you a deal" point of view, and they'll presumably use that gain to justify the purchase.

Chapter 5:

Gas lighting and Self Thinking

What is Gaslighting?

Gaslighting refers to a kind of psychological manipulation where a person makes you to doubt your reality, perception, memory and even sanity. It is a deliberate attempt at destabilizing and delegitimizing your beliefs using misdirection, persistent denial, lying and contradiction. Gaslighting gives the gaslighter a lot of power over you. As such, when an abusive partner has completely broken your ability to trust your own perceptions, you're likely to stay in an abusive relationship.

The term 'gaslighting' was derived from "Gas Light", a 1938 play that was later translated to a widely known movie "Gaslight" in 1944. In the play, the husband manipulates his wife by dimming the lights that were powered by gas in their home. When his wife points this out, the husband denies that the lights had changed. This made his wife to think she was losing her sense of reality to be able to send her to a mental institution and eventually steal her inheritance. Ironically, gaslighting happens at different relationship levels. It could be happening in your personal relationships where your spouse or parent is abusive, at professional level where your boss or even co-worker is constantly preying on you and in some instances by public figures like between a leader and his constituents.

When gaslighting happens between two partners, you're likely to dismiss the actions of an abusive partner as a harmless misunderstanding. However, the abusive behavior continues over time leaving you anxious, confused, depressed and isolated. This is in addition to losing sense of all that is happening to you. Thus, as a victim of gaslighting you start depending on your abusive partner more even in defining the reality around you thereby creating a very difficult situation to escape. In the case of parental relationships, gaslighting may manifest in the form of a parent who is always disapproving of the decisions of their child so that the child ends up questioning decisions they suspect their parent will not agree with. While the parent may or may not want to control the decisions of their child, they end up doing so by being overly critical. At school, gaslighting may happen when a popular student makes another to question their judgement of a situation or feelings.

Psychologists consider gaslighting to be a serious problem. Although Gaslighting can begin with small and seemingly negligible offenses, the problem is that the less significant instances where you get to question your reality or judgement usually have the potential of snowballing. Eventually, you find yourself in a cycle where you're unable to navigate through your day-to-day life with a clear, focused mind.

You also find it difficult to make decisions or even have a sense of well-being. When gaslighting happens, it's more of a power dynamic. That is, the person manipulating you wields some kind of power that leaves you terrified of walking out of or losing of the relationship. In some instances, you may be afraid of being seen as less than what you want to be seen as by others. As such, you may end up changing your perceptions so that you avoid having a conflict. The interesting thing about gaslighting is that the gaslighter may not necessarily have a malicious intention or even be aware that they are gaslighting another person. Instead, it could be a result of upbringing, where parents have strict beliefs and that is how the gaslighter perceives life. As such, recognizing that you're in a gaslight tango may not be straightforward as it may begin with extremely subtle ways and in most cases, it involves people who seems to care about you very much.

However, you need to be wary if you find yourself starting to question yourself a lot. Therefore, it's important to be aware of the red flags that you need to look out for to determine if you're a victim. This is the first step to getting out of it.

Signs of Gaslighting

One hard reality about gaslighting is that it can happen to anyone because it is done in a subtle manner that you can hardly realize that you're being brainwashed. Here are signs of gaslighting that you need to know:

Apologizing

When you are a victim of gaslighting, you will find yourself apologizing for just about everything. You may apologize for not doing things right and in the extreme; you could even apologize for your existence. The reason for this is simple; you most certainly see this as a way to avoid conflict with your aggressor. Even then, the apology is never a form of politeness rather a strategy to stay safe because you see it as a means of disarming the gaslighter. It is also a way of transferring shame from the narcissistic gaslighter to yourself hence minimizing the gaslighter's rage.

Second-guessing

This is another common sign of gaslighting that is a result of the erosion of your confidence. Thus, you're constantly living with the fear of making mistakes or compounding a situation that is already bad. It is common to find yourself asking what if and it reflects in the manner in which you solve problems or make decisions.

Absence of happiness and joy

When you are constantly exposed to the tactics of a gaslighting narcissist, you're likely to go through mental and physical torture resulting in a change of personality.

Consequently, you will begin feeling lonely, confused, unhappy and frightened. You could continue with this melancholic nature long after you have parted with your abuser.

Constantly asking 'Am I too sensitive?'

As a victim of gaslighting, you tend to become hypersensitive over time because of being humiliated constantly. You will be told you are 'too sensitive' countless times to the point that you start believing it.

You will then begin seeking approval before doing anything because you are afraid of making mistakes that will result in being humiliated.

Withholding information

As a victim of a narcissistic gaslighter, you often experience great shame and get tired of covering up the abuse.

Whenever friends and family members point out to you that you are being abused, you avoid the subject and eventually withhold information just to avoid conflict.

You know something is wrong but can't figure it out

The aim of gaslighting is getting to control and eventually influence your reality. Thus, when it happens you will be unaware of what is going on.

When you doubt your competence and reality, you become more dependent on the abuser. This becomes a vicious cycle that is confusing even as the gaslighter feels as sense of achievement.

Problems with simple decision-making

When you're entering into the narcissist's web of illusion and deception, you will not know the direction the relationship will go. As time goes by and you form a bond with the abuser you begin organizing yourself around their desires while giving up your authentic potential.

You will even begin to ask permission to do the most basic of things and lose the ability to make decision for yourself.

Consequences of Gaslighting

Gaslighting has a crazy effect that leads to exploitation, which you may hardly see. The emotional damage from gaslighting can be quite significant to the victim. More specifically, when you're exposed to gaslighting for too long, you lose your self-identity and instead develop mental and emotional concerns.

Although the consequences of gaslighting don't all come at once, they can be detrimental. They include the following:

Loss of confidence

One of the things that happens when you are subjected to gaslighting is erosion of your confidence so much so that you find yourself second-guessing just about everything. This is because your sense of self-doubt is heightened unreasonably so that every decision you make is punctuated by a "what if?". Moreover, you're constantly living with the fear of doing something wrong even as you become more sensitive to the constant lies, blame and humiliation from the narcissist.

Confusion

Constant exposure to the tactics of a gaslighter eventually make you bend your will. As a result, doubt creeps in your mind and with more gaslighting, you end up being confused by whatever is happening around you. While you will be aware that something is not right, you won't be able to figure out what it is. Confusion is usually a result of exploitation of your vulnerable self by the narcissist.

Indecision

One of the common outcomes of gaslighting manifests through questioning everything because you can no longer distinguish between what is real and what is imagined. Consequently, you will find it difficult to make choices even in cases that are straightforward because you don't know what is right or wrong.

You will be surprised how simple decisions like brushing teeth become difficult to make since you're caught up in an illusion. Instead, you will mostly align your choices and needs to those of the narcissist.

Melancholy

The long-term effect of gaslighting is that it takes away your joy and happiness. Through emotional abuse and mental manipulation, the gaslighter leaves you feeling lonely, confused, afraid and unhappy. You begin feeling that you are different from the carefree and confident person you once were.

When the gaslighter constantly manipulates you, you can develop a change of character. When the effects of gaslighting take a toll on you, you can have a change in personality that leaves you depressed.

Distrust

As a victim of gaslighting, you feel shame and strive to cover up the reality of mental manipulation that you're faced with even when family and friends begin to notice that there is a problem. Instead, you deny the subject or avoid the issue. You eventually begin to withhold information from well-meaning people because you live in fear of what will happen if the narcissist finds out. You begin to withdraw from society and distrust everyone else.

Interestingly, you not only have trouble trusting friends and family but also lack trust for yourself too. This makes it difficult to forge new friendships and relationships besides withdrawing from family and friends. This effect tends to be long term and may be experienced even when you have gotten the narcissist out of your life.

The Gaslight Effect

According to Robin Stern, the gaslight effect takes place when you get to point where you're often second-guessing your reality, are confused and not sure of what you think or even who you are.

Generally, gaslighting can be exasperating in the initial stages and destructive to the soul once it takes over. It takes a process to turn off the gaslight effect. Here are some six ways marshal yourself to stop the gaslight effect:

Acknowledge the problem

The first step is to recognize the problem by identifying whatever it is your partner does and how you respond to it. This will help you understand the situation and why you feel dissatisfied and disconnected in your relationship. This is an important step because it's common to feel misunderstood and lonely when you're a victim.

Have compassion for yourself

One of the harsh truths about gaslighting is that as a victim, you always feel as though you deserve it so you keep blaming yourself. This is a wrong approach. Therefore, you need to know how you're contributing to the problem and what you can do to make things right. Most importantly, be easy on yourself and know that you deserve to be appreciated and loved no matter how you feel.

Allow yourself to make a sacrifice

Walking out of a relationship means you have to pay a price. This may mean losing something you will never get to have again. Therefore, you need to evaluate the situation and determine if it's worth taking the risk after all before making a move.

Connect with your feelings

It's common to disconnect from your feelings when you're gaslighted. This is seen as a means of coping with the relationship. To disconnect from this gaslight effect, you need to express how you feel towards specific gaslighting events.

Empower yourself

Gaslighting often leaves you feeling incompetent and helpless; you feel like you can never do anything right. To break away, you need to begin tapping into your strengths by identifying your core competencies and abilities. When you know your visible strengths, you will have the courage to accept your inadequacies.

Make one move at a time

Taking action is powerful because it will empower you. You can begin by doing something good that you would not do ordinarily. It may mean taking a class or taking part in a charity. This is a great way of reclaiming yourself.

Ways to Turn Off the Gas

Now that you know the various ways to marshal the strength and will to turn off the gaslight effect, here are ways through which you can turn off the gaslight effect:

Separate truth from distortion

In most cases, the gaslighter will want you to believe their version of events that may have a small nugget of truth. This will make you believe everything they say as being the truth.

Therefore, being able to separate the truth is a crucial first step. Look at what the gaslighter is telling you through the lens of truth by comparing it to what it actually means.

Determine if a conversation is a power struggle and then opt out

It can be difficult to understand what your conversation with a gaslighter is about because the gaslighter is often trying to get an upper hand.

On the other hand, you that is being gaslighted are in a power struggle to win the approval of the gaslighter.

In a normal conversation, both parties will be willing to listen to each other and address emerging concerns even if it becomes emotional.

Identify the triggers

Take note of the situations that ignite the gaslighting process and avoid them. These may be certain actions, stresses, words or situations that leave you feeling threatened.

Pay attention to feelings as opposed to being right or wrong

Gaslighters often make accusations that have a tip of the truth to it. They exaggerate the reality to suit them while making you feel they're right. Thus, to stop this don't focus on who is wrong or right rather, pay attention to your feelings. If you experience genuine remorse you need to apologize. However, if you feel you've been bewildered or attacked it is a sign, you're experiencing the gaslight effect and need to disengage immediately.

Keep in mind you have no control over other people's opinions

You only have power over your thoughts. This means you can change other people's opinion even when you know what you're saying is right. Understanding this is a significant step towards attaining freedom from gaslighting.

Chapter 6:

The Art of Deception

What is Deception

Deception is not usually an easy theme to understand since it involves a lot of different things like for example distractions, propaganda camouflage and concealment. The manipulator is often able to easily control the subject's mind since the victim is often led to placing immense trust in this particular manipulative individual. The victims often believe in whatever the manipulator will say and might even be basing future plans and shaping their world base on the things that the manipulator is feeding their subconscious mind. This strong element of trust towards the manipulator can quickly fade away once the victim realizes what is going on. It is because of this very reason that a certain level of skill is needed for deployment of this theme, since only then will a manipulator be able to skillfully change the focus of suspicion towards him and onto the victim's paranoia.

In most cases, deception will often present itself in relationship settings and can lead the victim to have dominant feelings of distrust and betrayal between the partners in the relationship. This usually happens because deception is a theme that violates most of the rules of most relationships, together with having a negative influence on the expectations that come with the relationship. When getting into relationships, one of the things that are usually expected is the ease of having an honest and truthful conversation with their partner at all times. If the then learns that one of them is beginning to show signs of deception, they might have to learn the different ways using misdirection and distractions to pry out reliable and truthful information that they need from them. The trust would have gone into a permanent rift that will not be easy to come back from, since the victim will always be questioning everything that the partner will say and do wondering whether the story is actually true of fabricated. Most relationships will end as soon as the deceptive partner is found out.

Seeing as this the case, there are five main types of deceptive tactics that are seen to exist. We shall briefly touch on each one to better understand this theme.

Concealments

Probably taking home the medal of most used type of deception, concealment is basically when the deceptive individual knowingly omits information from his stories that are often relevant and important to the context. They can also engage in certain behaviors that would signal to hide of relevant information to the subject at that particular time. A skilled manipulator is experienced enough to know that he will have to be clever to know that it's safe not to be directly in their approach, but rather insinuate the lie leading the victim to their own conclusion which is predetermined.

Exaggeration

What can be said about this? This is where an individual in a sense stretches the truth a bit too much with an intended goal of leading the story towards a direction that best caters for their needs. The manipulator will make a certain scenario appear to be more severe than it actually is so as to avoid lying directly to their victims. This is usually done so as to let the victim do whatever it is, they want.

Lies

This is one tactic that we as humans use on a daily basis for one reason or another. We are often inclined to lie as a way to avoid some form of penalty. For example, if you work in the bank and you run late because of something minor, you will be inclined to lie to your boss so as to keep him from cutting you lose. What then can be said to be the meaning of this? This is where an individual gives information that is all south of the actual truth. They will present this completely fabricated truth to the victim and they will believe it.

Equivocations

This is where an individual will knowingly make a statement of a contra dictionary nature intended to lead the victim to the path of confusion on what is exactly seems to be going on. This is usually a clever tactic will allow the manipulator to save his image if he is later on discovered.

Understatements

This is where an individual minimizes aspects of the truth in the particular story being told at the time. They will often approach a victim preaching how something isn't that big of a deal, when in fact it is of the utmost importance.

Primary components of deception

As much as it may be a bit difficult to clarify which factors show clear deployment of deception, there are some subtle components that are immediate identifiers of these themes. The victim will come to be aware of these factors only when the manipulator dispatches a direct lie. Let us now dive deep into the particulars of said components.

Disguise

The first component we shall unravel is that of disguises. What usually goes on here is that the manipulator works tiredly up to until he successfully creates the impression of being someone that they are not. Manipulators often result in this tactic if they want to hide burry something about them so deep that no one ever finds out.

This could be a dark secret, or just something as harmful as someone's name. The popular belief of this component is that is simply a change of clothes just like in the moves, however it goes far beyond this in that it also involves a complete change of one's persona. Having a rough idea of how discuses work, let us look at a few examples of how it can be used in the process of deception.

The first instance is where the manipulator changes himself to another person so as not to be discovered. This will be done by an individual with a view to maybe be able to get back into a particular crowd of people that are not very fond of him, revamp their whole personality so as to make someone like them or just to further their own personal goals.in some instances, disguise may be used to refer to the hiding of one's true nature in the hopes of maybe hiding the effect that appears to be unpopular with that proposal.

Disguises usually have adverse effects because it is generally the hiding of one's true intentions for a particular victim. When information is withheld in this fashion, it often clouds the victim's judgment. The victim ends up having the feeling of being in control of their decisions when in reality they have been swayed towards the manipulator's directions. This is seen mainly in a political setting.

Camouflage

This is where an individual works tirelessly in order to hide the truth in one way or another leaving his victim clueless as to what exactly is going on. This is characterized by the manipulator's use of half-truths when divulging certain information to his victim. The victim will only be aware that camouflage has taken place later when the actual truths are brought to light. A skilled manipulator with a lot of experience using camouflage is more likely to bra undetected in performing certain actions.

Simulation

The third component of deception is what is commonly referred to as simulation. This is simply the process where the victim is constantly being shown subject matter that is false in every way. Further on, we get to see that simulation consists of 3 other techniques that can be used. They are mimicry, distraction, and fabrication.

Fabrication is the scenario where the manipulator takes something that is found in actual reality and chafes it to become this completely different thing. The manipulator will seek to either give detailed events of something that never happened or add some exaggerations that either make it sound better or worse than it actually sounds. The core of their story, however, is usually true. If the teacher gives them a bad grade, these manipulators may further the story by stating that they were given the bad results on purpose. The reality is that the manipulator did not study for the test hence his bad grade.

Mimicry is another tool that manipulators use when deploying these tactics of deception. The manipulator here usually portrays a persona that it is quite close to their own, but not their own. They may present an idea that is similar to someone else's and give him credit for thinking about it first. This form of stimulation may be able to take pace through visual and auditory stimulus.

The last tool we shall look at is that of distraction as another form of simulation in deception. This is where the manipulator tries to get the victim to only focus their attention on everything else but the truth. How is this usually done? This is usually achieved through baiting or the offering of something more tempting than the truth itself. The best example of this is that of a marriage situation.

Where the husband is involved in extramarital affairs and thinks that the wife has caught a whiff of this, he may start graving her with random gifts such as designer clothes so as to distract her from thinking about his cheating.th one flaw to this is that it often tends not to last as long as intended.

Detecting deception

If you may be interested in looking for the rights defenses against deception, then the first thing you would do is have a clear conscious that allows you to detect deception as its being deployed.it may be difficult in determining whether deception is occurring or not. This is of Corse unless the manipulator becomes a bit sloppy in his approach and levees sufficient breadcrumbs showing that he is indeed languor of grips contradiction of statements.as much as it may be difficult for a manipulator to deceive his victim for an extended period of time, it is something that we practice on those closest to us on a daily basis. What makes detection of deception a bit hard is that there are really no solid indicators that are 100% reliable to tell when deception has happened.

Deception, however, is capable of placing a large burden on the manipulators cognitive functioning as they will have to figure out how to recall the agent's functioning as they will have to figure out how to recall all the statements they made to the subject in order to keep the story credible and consistent. One slips up and the subject can say something is wrong. Due to the strain of keeping the story straight, the agent is much more likely to leak information to tip the subject through either nonverbal or verbal indications. Over the course of time, researchers have given us sufficient reason to believe that detecting an attempt of deception is usually a process that is cognitive, fluid and complex. These processes are not usually constant as they will often vary depending on the message that is being relayed. The interpersonal deception theory describes deception to be an iterative and dynamic process of influence between the manipulator, whose sole purpose of this is working towards twisting information to a version that best suits them but is different from the truth, and the victim, who will then attempt to figure out if the message being relayed to them is of an accurate nature or quite the contrary. It is during this particular exchange that the victim is going to bring to light all the nonverbal and verbal information that will cue the victim in to the deceit.at some point in this process, the victim may be able to tell that they are being lied to by the manipulator.

Chapter 7:

Hypnosis and Subconscious mind

What is Hypnosis

Hypnosis is when a person enters a state of mind in which a person finds himself or herself vulnerable to the suggestions of a hypnotist. Hypnosis is not new to us because many people have seen it in movies, cartoons or actually been to magic shows or performances where participants are told to do usual acts and they do it. One thing is for sure that, some people do believe that hypnosis actually exist and would do anything to avoid being a victim while others believe that its fiction.

Induction

Induction is considered as stage one of hypnosis. There are three stages in total. Induction is aimed at intensifying the partaker's expectations of what follows after, explaining the role they will be playing, seeking their attention and any other steps needed during this stage. There are many methods used by hypnotists to induce a participant to hypnosis. One of them is the "Braidism" technique which requires a hypnotist to follow a few steps. This technique is named after James Braid. First step would be to begin with finding a bright object and hold it in your left hand and specifically between the middle, fore, and thumb fingers. The object should be placed where the participant will be able to fix his or her stare and maintain the stare. This position would be the above the forehead. It is always important that the hypnotist remind the partaker to keep his or her eyes on the object. If the participant wonders away from the object, the process will not work. The participant should be completely focused on the object. The participant's eyes will begin to dilate and the participant will begin to have a wavy motion. A hypnotist will know that his participant is in a trance when the participant involuntarily closes his or her eyelids when the middle and fore fingers of the right hand are carried from the eyes to the object. When this does not happen, the participant is begins again being guided that their eyes are to close when the fingers are used in a similar motion. Where therefore, this puts the participant in an altered state of mind he or she is said to be hypnotized. The induction technique has been considered not to be necessary for every case and research has shown that this stage is not as important as previously had been known when it came to the effects of induction technique. Over the years, there have been variations in the once original hypnotic induction technique while others have preferred to use other alternatives. James Braid innovation of this technique still stands out.

Suggestion

After Induction, the next stage that follows is the suggestion stage. James Braid left out the word suggestion when he first defined hypnosis. He however described this stage as attempting to draw the conscious mind of the partaker to focus on one central idea. James Braid would start by minimizing the functions of different parts of the partaker's body.

He would then put more emphasis on the use of verbal and nonverbal suggestions to begin to get the partaker into a hypnotic state. Hippolyte Bernheim also shifted from the physical state of the partaker. This well-known hypnotist described hypnosis as the induction of a peculiar physical condition which increases one's susceptibility to the suggestions by the participant.

Suggestions can be verbal or one that doesn't involve speech. Modern hypnotist uses different form of suggestions that include nonverbal cues, direct verbal suggestions, metaphors and insinuations. Nonverbal suggestions that may be used include changing the tone, mental imagery and physical manipulation. Mental imagery can take two forms. One includes those that are delivered with permission and those that are done none the less and are more authoritarian.

When discussing hypnosis, it would be wise if one would be able to distinguish between the conscious mind and unconscious mind. Most hypnosis while using suggestions will try and trigger the conscious mind other than the unconscious mind.

While other hypnotists will view it as way of communicating with the unconscious mind. Hypnotists such as Hippolyte Bernheim and James Braid together with other great hypnotists see it as trying to communicate with the conscious mind. This is what they believed. James Braid even defines hypnosis as the attention that is focused upon the suggestion. The idea that a hypnotist will be able to encroach into your unconscious mind and order you around is next to impossible as according to those who belong to Braids school of thought.

The determinant of the different conceptions about suggestions has also been the nature of the mind. Hypnotists such as Milton Erickson believe that responses given are normally through the unconscious mind and they used the case of indirect suggestions as an example. Many of the nonverbal suggestions such as metaphors will mask the true intentions of the hypnotist from the conscious mind of the victim. A form of hypnosis that is completely reliant upon the unconscious theory is subliminal suggestion. Where the unconscious mind is left out in the hypnosis process then this form of hypnosis would be impossible. The distinction between the two schools of thoughts is quite easy to decipher.

The first school of thought believe that suggestions are directed at the conscious mind will use verbal suggestions while the second school of thought who believe that suggestions are directed at the unconscious mind will use metaphors and stories that mask their true intentions. In general, the participant will still need to draw their attentions to an object or idea. This enables the hypnotist to lead the participant in the direction that the hypnotist will need to go into the hypnotic state. Once this stage of suggestion is completed and is successful, the participant will move onto the next stage.

Susceptibility

It has been shown that people are more likely to fall prey of the hypnotist tactics than others will. Therefore, it will be noted that some people are able to fall into hypnosis easily and the hypnotist does not have to put so much effort while for some, getting into the hypnotic stage may take longer and require the hypnotist to put quite the effort. While for some even after the continued efforts of the hypnotist they will not get into the hypnotic state. Research has shown where a person has been able to reach the hypnotic state at some point in their lives then it is likely that they will be susceptible to the hypnotist's suggestions and those who have not been hypnotized or it has always been difficult for them to reach that state then it will be likely that they may never be able to reach that hypnotic state.

Different models have been established to determine susceptibility of partakers to hypnosis. Research done by Deirdre Barrett showed that there are two types of subjects that considered being more susceptible to hypnosis and its effects. The two subjects consist of the group of dissociates and fantasizers. Fantasizers are able to easily block out the stimuli from reality without the specific use of hypnosis. They daydream a lot and also spent their childhood believing in the existence of imaginary friends. Dissociates are persons who have scarred childhoods. They have experienced trauma or child abuse and found ways to put away the past and become numb. If a person belongs to this groups finds him or herself daydreaming, then it will be associated in terms of being blank and in creation of fantasies. These two groups will have the highest rates of being hypnotized.

Types of Hypnosis

A hypnotist can use different types of hypnosis a participant. Each of them will use different ways and will help with certain issues. Some types of hypnosis will assist in the area of weight loss while others will be used to help a participant relax. The types of hypnosis are discussed below.

Traditional hypnosis

This type of hypnosis is very popular and used by hypnotists. It works by the hypnotist making suggestions to the participant's unconscious mind. The participant that is likely to be hypnotized by this is one who does what he is told and does not ask many or frequent questions. If one was to self-hypnotize themselves, they will do this by using traditional hypnosis. Like we have said this type of hypnosis is very popular and this could be attributed to it does not require much skill and it is not technical. The hypnotist will just have the right words and just tell the participant what to do. This might pose a problem to the hypnotist where the participant is a critical thinker and is able to analyze a given situation.

Neuro-Linguistic Programming (NLP)

This type of hypnosis gives the hypnotist wide criteria for the methods they can use in the process of hypnosis. The hypnotist is able to save time during the process as the hypnotist will just use the same thought patterns as the one that is creating the problem in the participant. If it is stress for example, the same thought pattern causing this stress will be used to counter the stress. The different types of NLP are discussed below.

NLP Anchoring

This type of NLP can be used to motivation a person to accomplish their goals for example if they are trying to be healthier or trying to lose weight. The hypnotist will create a positive anchor that is in line with the mental image of the participant. The mental picture will be that of a sexy slim body. This image will be used as the motivator to start losing weight.

NLP Flash

This technique should only be done by a certified professional because it is considered to be very powerful and used to alter thoughts and emotions around the unconscious mind of the participant. It is considered helpful to persons who experience chronic stress or are addicted to a substance. Here is what the hypnotist will do; he or she where a person is addicted to a substance instead of it causing some feelings of happiness the act will now cause feelings of pain. Where the person had chronic stress, the cat will bring a sense of relaxation.

NLP Reframe

This is the third type of NLP that can be used in hypnosis. It aims and works well in helping the participant change the way they behave. The hypnotist, for this work, should be able to comprehend that there is in fact a positive outcome when the behaviour is changed. The focus on the outcome is critical as this is the reason for using this form of NLP in the first place. Despite this, the behaviour chosen to achieve the outcome is not as important. The process involves the hypnotist trying to engage with the unconscious mind of the participant. The end game is to get the unconscious mind to be responsible for the participant's new chosen behaviour that will help in achieving the secondary gain. This new behaviour will then be more acceptable to the conscious mind of the participant.

Ericksonian Hypnosis

This type of hypnosis uses stories and metaphors. This hypnosis uses stories and metaphors to create ideas and suggestions in the unconscious mind. This hypnosis is very effective and powerful but the only downside it has it is that it requires someone whose experienced and trained for it to work and be effective. What is the reason behind its efficacy? The reason underlying is that it is able to eliminate any resistance to the suggestions of the hypnotist. The metaphors used will be of two types. The first is called isomorphic metaphors. This is a common metaphor that gives steps to the unconscious mind by presenting s somewhat story to the participant that in the end will have a moral ending. The unconscious mind will be able to link the elements coming from the story and the element of the problem situation.

Learn Hypnosis and How to Use It

Once a person is under hypnosis, you can make suggestions. For example, you want a person to buy you something. You hypnotize them and suggest they buy it for you. Once they come out of the hypnosis, chances are they are going to get you what you suggested in the very near future.

Now, when you are using hypnosis in this way, you want to do it without the person knowing you are. You will not swing in a pendulum in front of their face to induce the trance state.

Be Powerful

You can create a hypnotic state for people by simply exerting power over others. Look at how people are likely to blindly follow a person who appears to be powerful. When you do this, you can get a following and the people following you will do what you say because they want to please you and stay in your presence.

You can use this technique among your friends, family and coworkers. Basically, any person that you have a pre-existing relationship with. You want to exert your power over time so that it does not feel too aggressive.

Once you notice you have followers, start small with what you are asking. They will do it without even thinking twice about it. Over time, you can ask for larger things and you will have no trouble getting them.

Mirroring

Now, the powerful approach works for people you know, but what about strangers? This is where mirroring comes into play. This allows you to quickly develop a rapport with someone once they see you both have someone in common.

This can almost put them into a trance because they will naturally like you and want to please you since they will perceive the both of you as very similar.

Use Stories

The right stories can put people into a trance-like state. Think back to when you were a kid and your parents would read you stories before bed. This would induce a deep state of relaxation. The same is true when you are an adult.

As you are talking to people each day, add in some anecdotes. This shows you on a more personal level and can even give you a sense of power and authority. You want people to be able to visualize what you are saying, so use imagery when you are telling your story.

Lengthy Speeches

When you want to induce hypnosis on a large group, lengthy speeches are the way to do it. Think about the television evangelists you have seen. They essentially use this form of hypnosis to get people to hand over thousands of dollars every time they hold a service.

When they are delivering their speech, they take few pauses. They use varied voice tones to annunciate points and keep people completely engrossed in what they are saying. They know what their message is, and they repeat it frequently. They often do it using different phrasing, however, so no one in the audience ever feels like something is being forced on them.

It is not uncommon for them to tell you exactly what to do without directly telling you to do it. When you are in this type of situation, you are so enamored with the speaker, that you will do just about anything they ask. They always present their lengthy speech and then they just pass the collection basket. They do not ask you to donate because they know you will because you feel dedicated to them.

Stacking

This is a hypnotic technique that works because you essentially overwhelm the people you are talking to. With this technique, you essentially bombard people with information. They are learning so many new things that they do not have time to sort through it. They do not feel they need to check facts because you are speaking with such authority that they automatically believe what you are saying. By the time you end your thoughts, you have essentially put them into a trance.

Eye Cues

When you are seeking to hypnotize, look at where their eyes are. If they are directly focused on you, you know that you have their undivided attention and you can start implanting ideas and suggestions into the subconscious.

Cold Reading

This is something that psychics use to convince people that they can actually read their mind and predict their future. You will start by making a vague statement. For example, if you know a person to be shy, you will state this. You know it is true and they will elaborate, giving you further information. You will use this further information to essentially make other predictions. Once a person feels that you have this almost clairvoyant ability, they are more prone to believe anything that you tell them.

Chapter 8:

Subliminal Persuasion

Subliminal persuasion

The word "subliminal" means underneath our consciousness. Subliminal persuasion means an advertising message that is displayed below the threshold of awareness or consumer awareness in order to persuade, persuade or help people change their minds without making them aware of what is going on.

This is about affecting individuals with more than words. Some of the subliminal methods of persuasion impact our stimuli with smell, eyesight, sound, touch, and taste. There are mainly 3 subliminal methods of persuasion to affect anyone. They are

Building a relationship-building relationship makes the other person feel comfortable. This will open up the other individual more. This can be accomplished through a healthy observation strength that matches their mood or state. This helps create confidence

Power of discussion

the power of a powerful convincing person is much connected to an advertiser's conversion. The correct words and inflections help you to be openly straightforward.

Suggestive power

Associating useful and desirable stuff in discussion or interaction enables an individual to become more open to fresh thoughts.

Suggestion and emotional intelligence

This stage may be described as having one central and dominant idea focused on the participant's conscious mind, which was to stimulate or decrease the physiological performance of the various regions within the participant's body. Later on, the use of different nonverbal and verbal suggestions was increasingly emphasized in order to convince the participant easily.

Achieve Optimal Persuasion with Subliminal Psychology

When you can expertly utilize the depths of a person's subconscious, your control over them is easy and vast. Subliminal psychology is one of the most effective ways to do this. Now, this is an advanced technique, so do not expect to become effective overnight, but know that with time and dedication, you will be able to start putting subliminal messages into the minds of those around you. Once you can do this, you will be able to control what they think and the actions that they take. Essentially, you become almost like a puppet master for those around you.

Subliminal Message Techniques

This is a type of message or affirmation that is presented either visually or auditorily that is sent in a way that is below what is considered to be normal for human visual or auditory perception. For example, a record might be playing on repeat, but you cannot really hear it with your conscious mind. However, deep in your subconscious, you are hearing it and fully registering everything that it is saying. In most cases, the messages used are meant to control you in some way or suggest that you do something.

For example, subliminal messages are commonly used in today's world to promote smoking cessation or weight loss. In general, you listen to recorded tapes with a specific message when you are sleeping. Your unconscious mind gets the message, but you never really hear it as your conscious self. Either way, research shows that it can be an effective tool to change your smoking or eating behaviors. You can use a similar technique to aid in changing how people think to make them more vulnerable to the types of persuasion that you prefer to use.

This is an effective way to control both your mind and the minds of others, but it can be a bit obvious when you do not use the techniques properly. As you read into the primary techniques, pay close attention to how you might introduce a person to them. This is important and ultimately your relationship with the person you are seeking to control will determine which of these techniques works the best.

Subliminal messages during sleep

This is one of the most common ways to use these types of messages. Most people will use them for themselves in this manner, but you can also use them with people you live with. For example, once you know your spouse is asleep, play a subliminal recording for about one hour. This is really all it takes to get your message across.

Now, it is imperative that you know for sure that they are sleeping or else you could do more harm than good to your persuasion efforts. When you create your recording, use a calm and steady voice. State exactly what you want the person to do.

Use no filler words. Use a maximum of 10 words and simply repeat it for the duration of an hour. Then, once the person is sleeping, play the recording at a very low volume close to their head so that their unconscious mind hears it.

Subliminal flashes

These do not take as long as they are not as risky as the above method. These are a type of visual subliminal message. You can create the flashes to say exactly what you want.

What is nice about this technique is that the message flashes so quickly that the conscious mind often does not see what it says. Only the subconscious is able to understand and record it. So, you are able to get some control over a person's mind without them knowing what you are attempting to control.

Unless the person you want to do this with knows about subliminal psychology, you can just tell them you want to show them something you created. It is best to do this on a computer so that the screen is large enough to catch and keep their full attention during the flashes.

Mixed subliminal messages

You can insert subliminal messages into the music or audiobooks that someone listens to on a regular basis. There are programs that can do this, so you do not have to be a tech expert to take advantage of this method. Just like with the subliminal messages during sleep, you will use a calm and steady voice. You want the messages to mix into the audiobook or music without being detected. Remember the subconscious mind will pick up on it even when they cannot actually hear it when they are awake.

Just make sure to use these messages in something they listen to daily, or almost daily. It is important that they hear it regularly in order to gain the most control.

Subliminal notes

This is the easiest method, but it is also the simplest to figure out if you are not careful. You can put messages inside messages throughout your home. For example, when you are creating the grocery list, add something else you want, but do not normally shop for. This puts the thought in the person's head when they are reading the list. This is ideal for smaller things that you want to persuade someone to think or do. So, keep it simple and use this method periodically. Unlike the above methods, it is not a good idea to use it every day.

Chapter 9:

How Persuasion impact our life?

What you can obtain through persuasion

Even after all this talk so far, you may be sitting there asking yourself why you'd want to learn how to influence people. Maybe you don't have all those problems I talked about, or maybe they don't bother you. After all, most people probably aren't fretting over the fact that they can't effectively use mind control techniques.

But that is precisely where they're wrong, my friend.

Persuasion is a very powerful and very valuable skill that not everyone has, but that everyone should have. It comes in handy throughout your life in virtually any aspect of your existence, from sweet-talking your way into free movie tickets to convincing your boss you deserve a raise.

In your personal life; Your relationship with your spouse

They say a good marriage or romantic relationship is all about compromise, but if you've ever been in a relationship you know that's not always possible. You have to pick one side or the other, and why wouldn't it be your side?

Far from being unfair or manipulative, having the ability to convince your significant other can actually improve your relationship because you have fewer fights about your disagreements and lack of compromise. Now you can use all that extra time and energy implementing your superior decisions.

Your relationship with your kids

Everyone knows that children are little demons. Infancy, terrible twos, teenage hood…they all come with a unique set of challenges, and they're all for you. Good job convincing your 3-year-old to get dressed when they're going through their naked phase, your 12 year-old to go to school, or your 15 year-old not to pierce their nose.

Having the persuasion skills and indisputable power and authority to convince your kids to actually do what you tell them to is as close to magic as you can possibly get. If you don't believe me, try it!

Your relationship with your friends

We all have that one friend who always makes terrible life choices, and no one can get through to them and steer them towards the right path…except you, that is. If you have influence and persuasion skills, don't keep them for yourself. Use them for good, not evil. Repeat after me:

"No, maybe you shouldn't marry that guy you just met."

"Yes, limiting your day drinking is a wonderful idea!"

"Please get that weird rash checked at the doctor."

"Stop stealing from your workplace, you're going to get in trouble."

Think of the difference you can make in someone's life!

In your professional life; Get paid what you deserve

Negotiating absolutely falls under persuasion, so really, absolutely everyone should have this skill. No matter if you're haggling at the market or discussing a higher salary, you need to have the ability to convince your 'opponent' that you deserve this, and you should have it.

It's mostly applicable in the workplace, where – let's be real – no boss will ever willingly part with their money and hand it over to you. So, it's your job to convince them to do it. You've earned it, you deserve it, and it's rightfully yours. You have to ask for it, but you have to know how, and persuasive skills help with that.

Earn the trust and respect of your boss

But of course, your only interaction with your boss isn't the yearly salary tug-of-war. If you're ever going to attain your career dreams and climb the corporate ladder, you need to have an excellent relationship with your boss, which means winning their respect and their trust.

You can accomplish that by becoming their go-to person. Offer your bright ideas, come up with solutions to problems the company is facing, persuade them to implement your suggestions and that they're the contribution the company needs right now. In time, you will reap the rewards when your boss comes to consult with your first.

Be a good leader to your colleagues

In order to be effective in any leadership position – whether you're a manager, a team leader, *etc.* – you need the power to convince people to:

a) Do what you tell them

b) Take you seriously

Obviously, your persuasive abilities will prove to be invaluable to a position like this if you want people to respect you, your work, and your ideas. It should be obvious for everyone that your way is the right way and there will be minimal dissent if you have the necessary influence over them.

In everyday life, get out of paying tickets

Legally, a ticket is a mandatory consequence of breaking the law in some way, by speeding, failing to wear your seatbelt, talking on your cell while driving, *etc.* Practically, however…a ticket can be a negotiation, as long as you have the necessary skills.

I'm not saying you have a free pass to going around causing mayhem, but if you have a busted tail light that you haven't gotten around to replacing and the coppers want to slam down the hammer of justice, some deliberate and convincing babbling capabilities can be very convenient. It'll never happen again, officer, you promise!

Get into coveted clubs or restaurants

How many times have you stood in line for hours to get into a popular club or restaurant, only to be turned away at the door by an unfriendly bouncer or snotty hostess? Well, let's see if you really need to have a reservation.

If you're persuasive enough, you can influence any menial gatekeeper and convince them to just let you through without needing to jump through fiery hoops or grease the well-meaning palms of anyone. Talk about some sweet perks!

Get important information

Do you feel like you're constantly being left out of the loop when it comes to important info among your family or group of friends? You don't have to try to guess what the drama is if you can just convince someone to tell you, even if they promised they wouldn't.

If you can talk the talk well enough, you can basically convince anyone to tell you anything. Gossip from your friend, preferred customer sales dates from sales attendants, where they keep the extra free peanuts from the flight attendant…you get the idea. Sweet talk yourself into perks and valuable info.

Conclusion

Thanks for making it through to the end of this book. Be on the lookout for those who may try to use some of these techniques against you.

If you are not on the watch, a dark persuader may be able to use these tactics against you, and you may never know.

You have to keep fighting your dark side so that it does not take control over you completely. Once you know to keep off that side on edge, you will be able to identify it in others and prevent yourself from falling prey to it.

You should be ready to get out there and get started with your newfound information that you have gained.

Don't let yourself be taken advantage of and learn that you, too, can fight back, protect yourself, and ensure that you can maintain yourself and your integrity.

Whether you are new to understanding persuasion or already victimized in the past, hopefully, you feel a bit more confident and in control! Good luck with your future endeavors and the growth that you will need to ensure your happiness!

References

Bandler, Richard and Grinder, John. *Frogs into Princes.* Edited transcripts by Steve Andreas. Real People Press, 1979. Web. 2 Dec 2017.

Cialdini, Robert B. *Influence: The Psychology of Persuasion.* HarperCollins, 1993. Web. 3 Dec. 2017.

Healthline. (2020). *Psychopath: Meaning, Signs, and vs. Sociopath.* [online] Available at: *https://www.healthline.com/health/psychopath#takeaway.*

Today, P. (2020). Changing behaviour with neuro-linguistic programming - Personnel Today. *[online] Personnel Today. Available at:* https://www.personneltoday.com/hr/changing-behaviour-with-neuro-linguistic-programming/.

Personality - Trait theories. (2020). Retrieved 2020, from *https://www.britannica.com/topic/personality/Trait-theories*

The Importance of Emotional Intelligence (Including EI Quotes). (2020). Retrieved 2020, from *https://positivepsychology.com/importance-of-emotional-intelligence/*

How to analyze people. (2020). Retrieved 2020, from *https://hubpages.com/education/How-to-analyze-people*

Explainer: how we understand people and why it's important. (2020). Retrieved 2020, from *https://theconversation.com/explainer-how-we-understand-people-and-why-its-important-26897*

Why is it important to understand personality? (2020). Retrieved 2020, from *https://preludecharacteranalysis.com/blog/why-is-it-important-to-understand-personality*

Mendoza, D., Mendoza, D., & profile, V. (2020). The Importance Of Being Able To See A Situation From Another Person's Point Of View. Retrieved 2020, from *http://danamendoza.blogspot.com/2011/11/importance-of-being-able-to-see.html*

Benefits of the Psychology of Personality. (2020). Retrieved 2020, from *https://www.ukessays.com/essays/psychology/benefits-psychology-personality-3099.php*

How to Read Body Language - Revealing Secrets Behind Nonverbal Cues. (2020). Retrieved 2020, from *https://fremont.edu/how-to-read-body-language-revealing-the-secrets-behind-common-nonverbal-cues/*

Parvez, H., & Parvez, H. (2020). Body language: Positive and negative evaluation gestures. Retrieved February 2020, from *https://www.psychmechanics.com/positive-and-negative-evaluation/*

^ *"Definition of 'Manipulate'"*. www.merriam-webster.com. Retrieved 2019-02-24.

Jump up to: *a* *b* *c* *d* Simon, George K (1996). In Sheep's Clothing: Understanding and Dealing with Manipulative People.*ISBN 978-1-935166-30-6. (reference for the entire section)*

Jump up to: *a* *b* *c* Braiker, Harriet B. (2004). Who's Pulling Your Strings ? How to Break The Cycle of Manipulation.*ISBN 978-0-07-144672-3.*

Kantor, Martin (2006). The Psychopathology of Everyday Life: How Antisocial Personality Disorder Affects All of Us.*ISBN 978-0-275-98798-5.*

Skeem, J. L.; Polaschek, D. L. L.; Patrick, C. J.; Lilienfeld, S. O. (2011). *"Psychopathic Personality: Bridging the Gap Between Scientific Evidence and Public Policy"*.Psychological Science in the Public Interest. *12* (3): 95–162.*doi:10.1177/1529100611426706. PMID 26167886.*

Frank, Prabbal (2007). *People Manipulation: A Positive Approach* (2 ed.). New Delhi: Sterling Publishers Pvt. Ltd (published 2009). pp. 3–7. *ISBN 978-81-207-4352-6.* Retrieved 2019-11-09.

Clancy, Frank and Yorkshire, Heidi. "The Bandler Method." *Mother Jones* Magazine. Mother Jones, 1989. 14(2): 26. Transcription of original article in Word document. 2 Dec. 2017.

Lee, Kevan. "189 Power Words That Convert: Write Copy That Gets Your Customer's Attention Every Time." Buffer, 2 Jul. 2014. Updated 1 Dec. 2016. Web. 2 Dec. 2017.

Real, Get. "38 Convincing Words and Phrases to Adopt Immediately." 38 Convincing Words and Phrases to Adopt Immediately—推酷. N.p., n.d. Web. 12 Apr. 2017.

Stollznow, Karen. "Not-so Linguistic Programming." *Skeptic*. The Skeptics Society, 2010. 15(4): 7. Web. 2 Dec. 2017.

Zetlin, Minda. "37 Words and Phrases That Immediately Increase Your Credibility." Inc.com. Inc., 16 Nov. 2015. Web. 12 Apr. 2017.

CPSIA information can be obtained
at www.ICGtesting.com
Printed in the USA
BVHW090308180521
607554BV00009B/1952